PEARLS WITHIN

PEARLS WITHIN
Empower Yourself To Make The Change

First published in 2014 by
Panoma Press

48 St Vincent Drive, St Albans, Herts, AL1 5SJ, UK

info@panomapress.com
www.panomapress.com

Book layout by Charlotte Mouncey
Printed on acid-free paper from managed forests.

ISBN 978-1-909623-67-5

A CIP catalogue record for this book is available from the British Library.

This book is available online and in bookstores.

PEARLS WITHIN

EMPOWER YOURSELF TO MAKE THE CHANGE

Samina Ali

This book is dedicated to my late mother;
it is in the most difficult journeys
that we see the best outcomes.

Acknowledgments

I firstly thank Allah the Almighty for giving me the ability and strength to write this book. I have a lot of people to thank for seeing me through this journey; firstly my husband who has been my backbone and a pillar of strength and has never given up on me. My three beautiful children were forever encouraging and assuring me that I could do this and I would not have been able to do it without their constant encouragement. I thank all my family and friends who have been continuously supportive on different levels throughout my journey.

I thank all the kind people who believed in me and took their precious time to review my book.

Finally I would like to thank my teachers Louise Baker and Mandy Martin and above all my coach Mindy Gibbins-Klein.

Contents

INTRODUCTION

For a couple of years now I have been saying that I need to write a book, not understanding why I had this feeling and also not knowing what it is that I wanted to write about, I just knew there was a message that I needed to share. Through my life experiences followed by my thought-provoking journey of studying hypnotherapy and psychotherapeutic counselling, my mind opened up to new intriguing avenues that it had never explored before. It touched profound depths which I was unaware even existed. My awareness of life, people, habits, behaviors, and personality types took on a new dimension as I learned to understand the existence and the birth of these aspects of people. I have always had an interest in the mind and the way it works as well as being intrigued by why people behave the way they do and how they come to make the choices they make, and the most important thing for me, the rationale behind people's thoughts and what is really going on behind the scenes, in the mind.

I firstly learned that I had to understand my own thoughts, behavior and personality, as this was intrinsic to what I wanted to do next, which was to do the same for others. Even though I ultimately wanted to help everybody better their life and gain an understanding of their journey, I identified a niche. The niche was very near to home, no further than within my own community, my own ethnicity. Coming from a Pakistani background and myself being a British Asian Pakistani, I noticed there was no real psychological depth in any part of my culture and it was much needed – but needed from someone who was one of them to truly understand and explain it in a language that could be understood. So I gathered that I did have important messages to share generally with them as well as more specific messages, and the best way would be to have it in the shape of a book, so it could be far reaching. Although saying this, the essence of this book can be applied to anyone from any culture and ethnicity, as beyond our cultures it is still the personality and behaviors around us that cause the greatest effect in molding us.

This book is about breaking the mold that we have inevitably adopted through our upbringing, impacted by the personalities of the authoritative figures around us at the tender age when the mind is like an empty memory stick ready to download any data and information from the world but not quite safeguarded to deal with viruses and their deep-rooted impact on the future. By no means is this book an exhaustive form on this topic, rather I would call it an introductory book to form a platform for understanding without getting completely overwhelmed. When learning the language of the mind, it can be quite mind-blowing, as if you were actually learning a foreign language. Therefore this book has been kept in its simplest form so it could be read from cover to cover without causing too much of an overwhelming effect, subsequently losing the reader's interest.

CHAPTER 1

WE HAVE ADOPTED OUR THOUGHT PATTERNS/BEHAVIORS FROM OUR BELIEF SYSTEM

Our belief system shapes us

Belief system is a set of beliefs that you have acquired about yourself and the world around you and which govern your thoughts. This is not a tangible system but a system of perceptions and impressions being developed in your mind from a very young age with all the data being recorded and stored in the subconscious part of your mind. Without realizing, all along this set of beliefs has been shaping you. This data which has been collected and stored subconsciously without you even trying and without awareness is made up of your experiences as a child with the people around you - usually parents, guardians and other significant adults. At a tender age the mind is like a sponge and starts soaking up whatever it sees, hears and understands around it and then starts storing this information, good or bad, in the memory bank of the subconscious mind. At this stage, right and wrong is not determined by a child's own mind but rather from what she is told and what she learns from the ones around her without the understanding of the possibility of ambiguity of what is seen or heard. I am sure we can all remember something we recall from our childhood that we believed to be something totally different from what it actually was when we think now with an adult mind. What about something that really terrified you as a child to the point that you thought this feeling of terror was going to take your breath away? For example, the first day of starting school, or when your mum had caught you taking two cents out of her purse for the gum machine. That same scene can be recalled in your mind now as an adult and you wonder what all the fuss was about.

Abdul's case study

> Abdul, a seven-year-old boy, was always praised by his parents when he did something good and when he behaved well and was told he was a very good boy. However, when he was naughty and deserved a telling-off for the naughty behavior, his parents made a point of explaining why he was getting told off and what was naughty about the behavior he was getting told off for. The action of his parents following "good" and "naughty" behavior with an explanation equips Abdul with the understanding of the difference between the

two behaviors. He could also associate rewards with the good behavior and no rewards for when he was naughty. We don't need to go into detail about what the good and naughty behaviors were as this is insignificant; what is significant is that the "good" and "naughty" behaviors which have been identified by his parents were differentiated for Abdul. He understood the difference between the two and the consequences of both. This positive conditioning by his parents was profoundly instrumental in the development of Abdul's belief system.

Imran's case study

Eight-year-old Imran, on the other hand, was constantly criticized by his parents on a daily basis and very rarely praised. When Imran was young and told not to kick the ball against the wall in the living room, he was also told he was a "naughty and stupid boy." This was never followed with an explanation of why he was naughty and stupid and why he should not be kicking the ball in the living room. That is fine, if that is the tone his parents wanted to apply with him; however, when Imran used to volunteer to help his mom lay the table for dinner, the volunteering part was not acknowledged but sadly what was acknowledged was when he accidently dropped the cutlery on the floor. The response from his mother following him dropping cutlery on the floor was exactly the same as when he was getting told off for kicking the ball in the living room: "naughty" and "stupid" boy. Again, no effort or time was taken to provide Imran with an explanation of why he was getting told off. He constantly repeated behaviors which subsequently got him into trouble as he cannot determine what is "good" and what is "naughty." This is all being stored in Imran's data bank, his subconscious mind, through what he is hearing, seeing and his understanding of it, shaping his belief system. Here you can see that Imran is not clear on the difference between a behavior that deserves scolding and a behavior that deserves praise. As far as he understands, both behaviors generate the same outcome, therefore it doesn't really matter which behavior he chooses.

We all have different shapes

We all have different shapes and our experiences shape us. Childhood experiences play a significant role in this and this is the factor that will determine which shape you develop into as an adult. Let's take a look at the different factors in childhood which are subconsciously molding you into a shape.

As children, we are told some things about ourselves as you can see with Abdul and Imran above; however, we are also learning things from the significant adults around us too which we can call learned behavior. This is how an angry parent's behavior is observed by a child and the child may begin to adopt these characteristics by watching this behavior often enough to assume that this is OK and normal.

Imran's case study

Imran also had a very angry father as far back as he could remember whom Imran's mom and sister were very scared of. Not only was Imran a victim of his father's anger but he was also observing and learning this angry behavior. He had seen his father use this anger far too many times to get his own way in things. Imran started to learn this behavior from his father and applied this subconsciously learned behavior throughout his life to get his own way too, never realizing where this may have stemmed from. So not only was Imran unable to differentiate between praiseworthy behavior and behavior deserving disapproval, but he was also a regular witness of anger, which he was subconsciously adopting.

Raj's case study

Raj had an abusive father who verbally and physically abused Raj's mother through his childhood right up until Raj was an adult and his father became terminally ill and was completely reliant upon Raj's mother. Raj had been watching this behavior day in and day out. He heard abusive language used around the house to address people and events. He also would physically abuse his mother by beating her if she was disobedient (disobedient in his eyes). Even though Raj was fearful of his father and his behavior and loathed it, it didn't stop him from subconsciously learning this behavior and applying it. His father was his primary male role model and therefore, even without trying, it was hard for Raj not to pick up this behavior.

Throughout Raj's childhood and growing up, it became normal for him to apply abusive language and aggressive behavior which led him into a lot of disputes and sometimes fights. Some of this is most likely learned behavior and some probably is a vent for the aggression from the events he had been witnessing.

Your shape can work against you

So we can see that the shape you have been molded into can work against you as well as for you. Being brought up with positive role models and praise and explanations can really help you get through life smoothly to some extent. However, this ideal world is not the case for everyone. Most of the

time, without realizing this, it is our shape that is holding us back in life. This is the shape that started being molded when we were children and the belief system was being developed.

Imran's case study

> Imran's childhood has left him with very little confidence and low self-esteem but extremely angry, which is holding him back in his true potential. Although he never obtained any solid qualifications, he has a lot of accountancy experience which he has gained through his current position at work. However, he cannot even build the confidence to apply for a higher position currently going at work which requires all the experience he has. This position would give him a better income than he has at present and better prospects for the future. This has always been the case for Imran so he has remained in the same position for 12 years and does not have the confidence to think he can try to apply for a higher position. On the other hand, at home, his anger problem is having a profound effect on his relationship with his wife and children. Imagine this was not Imran's shape: he could have used his full potential and excelled with his accountancy experience, and he could have attained a higher position at work. The company is even willing to pay the course fees for the qualification required for the position. At home, Imran could have a bet-

> ter relationship with his wife and kids. Chances are that his children will observe his behavior like he observed his father's and learn it subconsciously, just like he subconsciously learned his father's, and the cycle will start again.

Raj's case study

> Raj's learned abusive behavior has gotten him into a lot of trouble through school and college life and consequently held him back from progressing in life. He is now a bachelor at the age of 42 with no set job or career prospects and no real commitment to anything. He has an ongoing history of drug abuse which he cannot seem to overcome.

Your shape can be modified

Reading the above probably made you think: *This is it, I do not stand a chance, and the damage is done for life*. Well, rest assured, this is not correct. The damage was being done up to now, but that is it; from this moment onward this can change. When I say this, I mean the negative patterns and behaviors in your life, the negative shapes.

One of the reasons why this pattern of behavior molded in these shapes is perpetual and continuous is a result of something called CCF: Conscious Critical Faculty. This is an internal filter we use to interpret how the world works based on all we have learned since we were born. It is the part that helps us get through life with the understanding about things based on what we have been taught; for example, we are taught that the sky is blue and similarly we are told a lion is dangerous. As this is imbedded in our subconscious now, if we are told the sky is green or the lion is a very friendly animal, our CCF will reject it. We interpret the world through this filter and we accept information that conforms to our beliefs created in our belief system, and quickly reject or dismiss any information that opposes our view of the world. Therefore our subconscious mind, which has been absorbing the negative comments others have made about us at that sensitive age when the belief system was being created, rejects it when it hears something opposing it because the CCF rejects it. The subconscious mind is a composite of everything one sees, hears and any information the mind collects that it cannot otherwise consciously process to make meaningful sense. The conscious mind cannot always absorb disconnected information, as it would be an information overload, so the subconscious mind stores this information where it can be retrieved by the conscious mind when it needs to defend itself for survival.

Isla's case study

When Isla was growing up, she was constantly told that she was fat, by her parents, uncles and aunts. As she has grown up believing this and the subconscious mind has accepted this to be the truth, it will reject anything that it hears which is contrary to this. In her teens, when Isla was told how pretty she was by some of her peers, her mind rejected it as their comment did not fit the picture created of her by her parents, uncles and aunts in her mind. This has held Isla back in school from participating in certain activities especially sports as she thought she was too fat and held a belief of sports being for slim people. She also had stage fright at school for the same reason and the fear of being laughed at.

Daniel's case study

Daniel had a speech defect as a child (lisp) which meant he experienced difficulty pronouncing a few letters because of incorrect tongue placement and was picked on by his father a great deal. His father told him this was a girly problem and does not suit a boy. This had a profound negative impact on Daniel's confidence and he very rarely participated in class group activities. He had very few friends and would not take chances to even make friends due to lack of confidence in himself. He would also exhibit odd behavior like picking on the girls, just to prove that he was a boy and different from girls.

At the age of seven, fortunately he grew out of his lisp, but his father's view of Daniel was never modified. Every time his father needed to tell Daniel off he would still revert back to the time when Daniel had a lisp. He would start to call him offensive names alluding to his former speech problem.

Daniel excelled in his learning but kept holding himself back because he believed he wasn't good enough and neither was his speech. He also fought within himself not to appear clever and answer all the questions correctly as that might seem "girly," supporting his father's perception of him. He was very satisfied when he achieved acceptable grades for most classes at school. This facilitated him with the power that although he could not control his father's perception of him, he could however control his own achievements. His teachers at school tried to push him but this was an abortive attempt as Daniel had made up his mind of the level of achievement he wanted. He always knew that his teachers knew this was not his true potential.

Whenever he was praised and it was explained to him how he had the potential to be sitting higher papers for his exams etc. his mind would completely reject this as it did not correspond with the perception created in his mind by his father, and his CCF would reject anything that opposed this. He continued on in life like this and through into his employment where he was always recognized to have the potential but not the back-up of confidence.

Modifying your shape

Step 1

The first step to modifying your shape is recognizing it and its roots. When I say roots, I mean doing a good self-search of your history, even if you have to write it down and link back to where certain negativities originated from.

Who was around you when you were a child who may have influenced your shape?

At this point don't think *They didn't mean to* or *They meant well*, we will deal with that part later.

At this point just do the linking and see if you can recognize:

- *Your shape*
- *Where it took its shape from*
- *Who helped shape it*
- *Finally, what shape you would have liked to be*

One way of doing this is by drawing out a timeline of your life. The timeline could contain peaks and dips at times of peaks and dips in your life. But this is not a standard timeline which will just show the occurrences over time in your life with the peaks and dips; instead the dips need to have branches linking to the significant adults around you at that time and a further branch extending from each adult showing their positive/negative impact on you. You could do this exercise in different ways, whichever is easiest for you. Another way could be to draw a map and see if you can link up certain parts of your shape to any significant adult in your life from childhood to now. Take your time in doing this. You may surprise yourself with what you unravel here and where the links are. I don't want you to worry too much about how to do this exercise right and I don't want to elaborate too much on one particular exercise as I believe in flexibility. We all are different and learn in different ways; what works for one does not necessarily work for another, and this book is about you, not about putting you off from moving on to the next chapter because you feel you cannot resonate with a particular exercise. Therefore there is no pressure and there are no set exercises, just a little guidance on how you could perform this task to see links.

Step 2

Once you are satisfied with your maps and timelines and you have established the links, look at them and notice they all have a story to tell.

- *Anything positive leave aside as that does not need modifying unless you want to improve it further.*
- *Take each part of the shape and its link, one at a time, and take it a step further by exploring who said what, and how that made you feel.*
- *Identify the effects of this in your life now.*

This is a very personal exercise and therefore you can be completely honest with yourself, and I can assure you that the more honest you are with yourself, the more benefit there will be in this. The reason why we think twice about talking to people about the effect such-and-such had on our life and how it made us feel is due to the fear of exposing our vulnerability, so we rather keep things suppressed. But this is different because you are not speaking to someone, neither is anyone going to read what you are writing. Therefore this is your opportunity to be completely honest with yourself.

Step 3

Once you can see the link and the effects it has had on your life, you can start to think of what you would like to do with it. Remember this is your opportunity to empower this shape molded by others to give it a new better shape.

The ways in which this can be done are:

- *Assessing the shape induced by each link and modifying it to how you would have wanted it to be. I know this sounds like a click of a button called* **'MODIFY'** *or are you just supposed to wave a magic wand over it? No, not at all. You are just going to establish a modified shape required of your choice for each link established and write it or visualize it – whatever works for you.*

- *Identifying what is required by you to get to that stage. Some stages may have a few stages before them to get to that stage; don't let this put you off as you know that to get to every stage, there are always some steps to climb first. This is a good sign as you have established further layers in need of modification.*

Don't be hard on yourself; try each link in turn, and if further layers are established, work through them one at a time. Don't try to be a martyr and try to change everything in one go because the likely chances are that you will not change anything at all and this will be a fruitless task. You want to be able to enjoy this and feel a sense of achievement and reward with each little achievement. Why shouldn't you, considering you are doing two really important things: firstly helping yourself to achieve a better quality of life and secondly working hard to be green? When I say green I mean you are not wasting yourself, rather you are recycling yourself to save the earth from further pollution of character.

YOU ARE RECYCLING YOURSELF TO SAVE THE EARTH FROM FURTHER POLLUTION OF CHARACTER

CHAPTER 2

WE ALL INTERPRET A SITUATION DIFFERENTLY

Interpretations can come from different sources

There are many sources from which interpretations can be derived. We may all be looking at the same sky but have completely different interpretations of what this means to us. For some the beautiful blue sky with a few white clouds may seem as if the sky is calm. To another it may seem as if the sky is beautiful but has a few threatening clouds.

A mother telling her child off in a supermarket for attempting to buy a toy may seem to one person that the mother is being horrible to the child. To another it may seem like the child is being greedy and the mother does not know how to control it. From another angle it may seem that the mother is treating the child unfairly and there is nothing wrong with the child wanting that toy. Little do any of these interpretations understand that the mother is actually trying to discipline her child to be allowed to buy a toy as a treat for good behavior, and in this instance this was not the case.

You must be wondering why it is so important how we interpret a situation - after all, everyone has a right of opinion and freedom of speech. Well, it is not to do with any of these, rather it is a means of measuring a state of mind, which can work for you and against you. A healthy mind will always work for you to provide you with peace of mind and soul, while an unhealthy mind will be like a closet full of clutter.

The way we interpret a situation can also have a profound impact on the kind of choices we make in our life as well as our relationship and interaction with others.

Coming back to our belief system, this plays a major role in how we interpret a situation. Our primary interpretation of the world is fostered from our belief system and, as seen in Chapter 1, this can have a profound effect throughout our life until modified.

Abdul and Imran

> Abdul's interpretation of the world generally will be that good behavior is rewarded and inappropriate behavior has penalties as this was what he

> had learned from his parents. On the other hand, Imran sees the world as a place of punishment. You will get punished whether you do good or bad. He doesn't even understand the difference between good behavior and bad behavior as this was never differentiated for him as a child. His understanding is that you will never please anybody, therefore don't even try. This last point has affected his relationships significantly as he does not class any relationship to be worth trying for or fighting for, rather he employs a subconscious policy of use and abuse and move on.

Culture has a very interesting effect on how we interpret a situation. Whether it is the culture you have been brought up in at home, the culture at school or the culture of the society you live in, all have a hand in your interpretation of the world. Therefore the culture you have been brought up in essentially sets the boundaries for how you might choose to see and interpret a situation.

If you were brought up in a household where you do not raise your voice to your parents, you then one day witness a child having a constructive conversation with his mother at the same level as himself. You may immediately interpret this as the child having no respect for his mother and see it as a child disobeying and arguing with his mother.

Children inherit a lot of culture from the schools they attend. This is a different kind of culture from the culture they are being brought up in at home. Here they have learned certain morals and conduct of behavior adhering to the school policy. They know they have to line up when told, eat at lunchtime, play at times allocated, respect the teachers and they also know the consequences of not adhering to this. This culture has started teaching the child at a very young age about rules and behavior and rewards and punishment. When a child sees home life in contrast to this and then sees their parent or parents being abusive toward him, he can very easily interpret this as a punishment from the understanding taken from the culture learned at school.

What about the society we live in, surely that must have an impact too on our interpretation of the world?

Sophie's case study

> Sophie was the only black child in her neighborhood when she was young. The town she lived in had very few ethnic minority residents. Racism was a common and normal reaction in the town to anyone who did not fit the ethnic criteria for the common British white person. Sadly, Sophie

was a victim of verbal racist abuse throughout her childhood as well as physical bullying at times. Being a victim of this through her childhood has left Sophie feeling insecure about her heritage. She would rather lie about herself to fit in than induce racist behavior toward her. She has grown up believing that everyone lies to protect themselves, therefore she has never really been able to trust anyone. The result of this has been that she has made herself a recluse and consequently reduced the chances for herself to have concrete relationships with friends and work colleagues.

Unfortunately, dysfunctional life experiences can sometimes place a permanent default interpretation of the world or a situation.

Isma's case study

Isma split up with her husband after many years of arguments and fights over him being lazy and not working and earning and supporting the family. Because of this unfortunate experience with her husband, Isma believes that all men are the same: they are lazy and cannot support a family. She refuses to even think about another man let alone another marriage as if all men are diseased with this disposition.

Raj's case study

> Raj watched many years of his father's abuse toward his mother and felt the world would be a better place without him. He doesn't really take to male authority figures and tends to shy away from them; he would rather work for a female boss than a male one. This is probably relating to his experience with his father who has made him hesitant of male authority figures, giving him the negative feeling or memory of him being made to feel inferior and vulnerable. Ironically his father's negative influence has made Raj an abusive person too, and as much as he despises his father's behavior, he has perpetuated all his father's errors and flaws. Therefore Raj feels he can apply abuse to get his way as did his father.

Interpretations can be different

Individual life experiences impact how we interpret a situation, an event or even a person. Therefore two people looking at the same event, situation or person can interpret what they are seeing or understanding completely differently. I am sure we can all relate to this and cannot understand why someone else is not seeing what we are seeing. This doesn't mean either is incorrect, it just shows that this is possible, even when the subject is the same.

There are many reasons why interpretation can be seen from different perspectives and there are factors that influence this. Firstly, our childhood experiences will without doubt influence how we view and understand things. A healthy upbringing will provide you with a platform for a healthy perspective and understanding of a situation as well as being able to understand an unfortunate event. By this I mean you have the ability to understand that everything isn't always happy and that unfortunate events happen too and that this is part of life. This is because we can interpret a situation or event based upon our own experiences, and an unhealthy and dysfunctional upbringing can give you a negative perspective of situations or interpretations based upon your own experiences.

Example of different interpretations of the same event

> Abdul witnessed a conversation between two men at a bus stop, where one man questioned another man about his dress code and why he was wearing a thobe in the UK being a western country. A thobe is an ankle-length garment, usually with long sleeves, similar to a robe. It is commonly worn in Iraq and Arab countries bordering the Persian Gulf. The man who was asked gave his answer which then incited further conversation. As Abdul watched, he was intrigued to see how this man

had a lot of interest not only in the fact that an eastern thobe was being worn but also that the man wearing it appeared very confident to wear it.

From another perspective Imran was watching the same conversation and it instantaneously made him defensive, and he immediately assumed this man was being bullied about his dress code. He wasn't going to have it and was getting hyped up to sort this man out as well as having conflicting thoughts in his mind as to why the man wearing a thobe was not defending himself and telling the other one to mind his own business. Is this really what was happening? Yes, in Imran's case it was but not in Abdul's case. They are both seeing the same situation but from completely different lenses. Imran's aggressive interpretation can be linked back to his experiences mentioned earlier.

The above is an example of what happens to us on a daily basis, when more than one person is looking at the same situation yet interprets it completely differently. This is where our life experiences influence how we see and interpret things.

Social status

Social and economic factors can influence our interpretation too. Someone who had an advantaged upbringing may interpret a situation differently from someone that was less advantaged. A less advantaged person may look at a disastrous event on TV about a country undergoing war or a natural disaster and really feel their pain but not have the means to make a donation. On the other hand, a more advantaged person will see the same event and have the means to make a healthy donation, yet on a personal level this is just a natural disaster in their case and therefore as protocol money should be donated to show your support. Again, it is not that one is wrong and the other is right, but rather how their social status can impact their interpretation of this event.

There is no default in how you interpret something; difference of interpretation is OK unless harmful to yourself or anybody else. Like in Imran's case, where he could have caused an argument with the man talking about the thobe, accusing him of discriminating against the dress code of the man wearing the thobe, and in like manner he could also have been annoyed with the man wearing a thobe for not defending himself.

It's OK to be different

Yes, it is OK to be different as long as it is not unhealthy and causing you to be unhappy and untruthful to yourself, and provided it is socially and morally acceptable.

Why do people shy away from being different and having a different interpretation, and feel the importance of being uniformed in what they see and how they want to be understood? What does "different" mean to us? We seem to feel safe around what we call like-minded people because it is easier to "gel" with them. Just like it is comfortable to be what everybody else is being, otherwise being different will be too much effort to explain and justify and furthermore to maintain. Most of the time, the people we think are like-minded may not actually be like-minded but instead we have adjusted ourselves to fit their disposition which we are comfortable with, because we don't have the confidence to openly display our own disposition.

Having a different interpretation can be scary on many levels. Being different from what we think is expected of us makes us feel that we won't fit in. What does "fitting in" mean though? It doesn't have to mean that everybody has to think and be the same – surely that would make the world a boring place to live in. We are too scared sometimes to step out of the box of what our family, friends and peers are doing or saying for fear of not being accepted. There is also fear of being laughed at. I think one of the biggest reasons people are scared to be different or have a difference of thought and opinion is because as a child they were never given the confidence of independent thought. As a child they may have had their confidence knocked right down to the ground when an independent thought was applied by them as a child but rejected by the parent. Parents often laugh at their children's independent thought, without realizing that a moment of laughter for them could be a lifetime of permanent damage for the child. The thought process applied by the child to initiate an independent thought, whether it is to offer to help in the kitchen, lay the table or even put items in the shopping trolley, has had very little effort put into it but the immense damage that can generate from a parent ridiculing the child can be quite astonishing.

Abdul and Imran

> Abdul is not scared of putting his own interpretation of a situation across even though it can be completely different from others' at times. This is because as a child he was given the ability and confidence of independent thought. He doesn't fear being laughed at as he is confident in what he says.

> Imran often interprets things differently from others but he does not have the ability or the confidence to express the difference of opinion confidently, rather he would settle for an aggressive approach to his difference of opinion.

Therefore it is not just about having or not having different interpretations, it is also about having the confidence to communicate them. Until communicated, you will never learn to understand if your interpretation is "acceptable," even if different, or if your interpretation needs modifying to become acceptable. What I mean by acceptable is firstly that you are comfortable with it and secondly that you feel comfortable about the way people have received it. Therefore you will never know that it is OK to have a different interpretation until it is communicated and practiced.

Did you know your different interpretation of an event or situation could be the light bulb?

Mr. Briggs and Ryan

> Everybody had noticed that recently Mr. Briggs in Ryan's neighborhood is causing a lot of problems by not clearing his front yard and allowing his garbage to fly across everybody else's front yards. Ryan and many other residents in the neighborhood have approached him about this issue and

Mr. Briggs would say that he will clear it soon. After enduring this for some time, a neighborhood meeting is called and it concludes that another three days' chance are given to Mr. Briggs and if he fails to comply and clear his front yard then a formal complaint will be forwarded to the Council with all the local residents' support. While Ryan was listening to everybody singing from the same hymn sheet, it suddenly occurred to him that Mr. Briggs has never done anything like this before in the time Ryan has lived here, and that there could be a justifiable reason for it. At this point Ryan felt that it would appear silly to mention what was brewing in his mind as he would stick out like a sore thumb. However, he decided to go ahead and say how strongly he feels that Mr. Briggs has never been the subject of any complaint in the neighborhood for the 12 years he has resided there and maybe there is a reason for this. He asked the neighborhood attendees if he could pop round to see how Mr. Briggs was doing and to determine if there was a change in his circumstances that was causing this. Much to Ryan's surprise, everybody said they thought that was a wonderful idea and they had never thought to look at it this way. Ryan's different interpretation was the light bulb of that scenario as, following that, it transpired that Mr. Briggs' health had deteriorated and this subsequently impacted his daily tasks. Mr. Briggs told Ryan that he found it difficult to tell this truth to the residents, as no one asked the reason for the garbage in the yard, rather they would just come and start complaining.

Nelson Mandela was a man among many in the same situation, seeing the same as others yet having his own interpretation, which he pursued subsequently making him a legend.

At his 1964 trial, Mandela chose to make a speech rather than testify. These are the closing words:

"During my lifetime I have dedicated myself to this struggle of the African people. I have fought against white domination, and I have fought against black domination. I have cherished the ideal of a democratic and free society in which all persons live together in harmony and with equal opportunities. It is an ideal which I hope to live for and to achieve. But if needs be, it is an ideal for which I am prepared to die."

His genius was in his pragmatism, his generosity of spirit. What set him apart from his fellow detainees was that he was wise enough to be influenced by new ideas and in turn was able to soften and broaden the minds of other young radicals, helping him recruit activists from opposing ideologies to the ANC (The African National Congress is the

Republic of South Africa's governing political party). http://www.bbc.co.uk

Interpretations need to be healthy

All interpretations are correct in the sense they are interpretations of how you are seeing a particular subject or a situation. They are how you perceive the world to be from your point of view from your experiences. However, not all interpretations are healthy.

Sara's case study

> Sara held it against her parents that they never provided her with the luxuries some of her friends had. She was always wearing hand-me-downs from her sisters and rarely had the opportunity to buy something just purchased solely for her. She also cannot forgive her parents for the fact that she was never allowed to go on school trips when all her friends were going. There were many occasions when she felt deprived in comparison to her friends and hated her parents for making her feel this way, holding them fully responsible. She grew up with the interpretation that her parents stole her childhood from her and deprived her, and subsequently made her bitter especially toward her parents, and parents in general. She adopted

> a belief of "earn lots of money and never have children until you can afford every luxury for them."
>
> Through therapy she started to understand that her parents struggled significantly financially and were not able to provide their children with what a lot of the other parents could. She then started working on having a healthy interpretation of her parents and began to understand that they did the best they could in their situation and were in fact very loving parents. This change of interpretation helped her cope and water down a long-burning fire and helped her make peace with that area of her life.

Changing an unhealthy interpretation to a healthy one will help you move on and have peace with your situation. It will also help you to understand that one story or event can have many different perspectives, as well as the importance of settling with a healthy perspective.

As there is such a fine line between this chapter and the next, there will be an exercise to follow in the next chapter that will apply to what has been covered in this chapter.

CHAPTER 3

WE ALL HAVE OUR OWN PERCEPTIONS OF SITUATIONS

Perceptions are the way you see the world

Perception is our sensory experience of the world around us and involves both the recognition of environmental stimuli and actions in response to these stimuli.

Perception is not tangible, rather it is how you see something to be. There is a thought process that goes into how you perceive something. When you see or hear something before your mind makes an assessment of what you perceive it to be, the mind goes through a mini thought process. It firstly compares this situation, person or whatever the subject may be to similar past experiences. If this feels or sounds the same, then likely chances are you will see this subject in the same light. If in the past this caused fear or threat, likely chances are it will cause the same emotions and feeling again. If it was associated with happiness or calmness, then likely chances are you will see it in the same light again. Most of the time this thought process takes place subconsciously and you are not aware that the mind is going through a process to make an analysis or judgment. A perception can work for you as well as work against you.

Perceptions can come from many different sources

How one sees a situation, meaning its perception, can come from many different sources. There seems to be a fine line between interpretation and perception, although perception is more the act of perceiving by means of the senses of the mind, cognition and understanding, while interpretation is more how we have understood something and then translated it.

Your life experiences play a significant role in how you perceive a situation. Positive life experiences will help in perceiving things in a positive accurate light with room for variability and ideas because it has that positive foundation behind it. Negative life experiences can make you perceive a positive situation as a negative one.

Raj's case study

Raj's experiences have geared him to perceiving situations to be victim/culprit kind of scenarios. When he perceives a scenario or situation, he usually subconsciously starts to find a pattern of a victim and a perpetrator as that is how his experiences began with his father being the perpetrator and Raj's mother continuously being the victim of his abuse.

The subconscious mind soaked up these early childhood experiences when the belief system was still being created to now conclude that this is how life generally is. Therefore based upon this platform of experience, he naturally assumes and perceives all situations to be like this. His scenario shows the profound impact early life experiences can have on our perception of the world.

Isma's case study

Isma's separation from her husband has convinced her to believe that men are generally useless. In any given scenario where there is a man or a relationship involved, she assumes by default that the man is at fault. Her negative experience with her husband was an experience for her. Yes, others go through similar experiences and a lot of couples separate but this does not translate that all men are from the same category as her husband and neither does it mean that all relationships will end up like hers. This has become a little dangerous as her perception has been rubbing off on to her friends, where before she could be quite objective but now she perceives all situations regarding relationships negatively and finds the men at fault.

Shan's case study

Shan was brought up with a very strong cultural upbringing and was always obedient to her parents. Her abiding by this strong cultural upbringing brought lots of joy to her parents and therefore she continued. She never really had her own opinions or views but instead these opinions and views were given to her on a plate without choice and she would just accept them. It wasn't that she was unhappy with this upbringing, she felt quite comfortable as her submissive attitude brought a lot of joy to her parents. The cultural grounding became so dominant that she could not even think for herself. A few times when she did try to be innovative and think for herself at the age of 14, when she experimented by asking her teachers if she could drop Spanish and take up French, she was immediately rebuked by her parents, causing them to be upset that she was not trusting her parents' choices. Another time when walking home from school with the same friend she always walked home with every day, Shan asked her friend if she would like to pop into her house until the rain had stopped as it was so ferocious. Again she was rebuked by her parents for this as she did not seek their permission and consult with them and it went against their beliefs that friends are to be kept out of the house and not brought home. She explained to them that it was not possible to seek their permission as the rain had come down hard at that time and naturally she thought to shelter her friend as her friend did not have an umbrella in her possession and she had a bit of a walk until she would reach home. Shan didn't enjoy the few experiences she had of being innovative and the reaction it generated from her parents, therefore she settled for a more viable attitude toward life, driven by her parents' decisions and choices, which were driven by their strong cultural values and beliefs

The problem started when Shan became a teenager and from there onward. When she witnessed anything her friends or peers were doing which she knew her parents would not approve of, even though it had nothing to do with them and there was no harm in it, she would consider this as not acceptable. This went right down to the fact that she often made judgmental remarks at peers and friends resulting in her becoming less popular around her peers.

Shan journeyed through life into adulthood being a very judgmental individual. She would perceive each situation and person through the lenses that were prescribed to her by her parents and saw the world through these prescription lenses and quite happily sailed through life like this. As early adulthood kicks in, you generally begin to switch to your self-prescribed lenses; however, not in Shan's case because she molded into the lenses prescribed by her parents.

Abdul's case study

Abdul perceives the world differently than the two mentioned above. He wouldn't perceive every situation with one default mindset. As he had the experience of being praised when doing something good, and was also provided with an explanation of why he was being scolded when doing something which was considered inappropriate, this has equipped him with the ability of understanding that there is flexibility in perceptions in different situations.

He perceives the world to be a means to grow and learn from. His perception is variable depending on the scenario or the person. There is no negative default mindset that has set a platform for his perception of the world. Rather his default setting of the perception of the world is that everything is flowing and is variable depending on each scenario and each person. This healthy mindset can help Abdul make healthier assumptions and perceptions allowing this to impact the world around him. This is in no way saying that Abdul is perfect and has the perfect life, as I am sure you would agree that this is not the case for many. It is showing that he is equipped to deal with life's ups and downs without a negative backdrop hovering over him to influence his perception of the world.

Isma's case study

We have seen above that Isma's separation from her husband has geared her with such a negative perception of any similar situation. This has subsequently led to her impacting or instigating further relationship break-ups when people were relying on her perception of a situation for advice. Further, this could run in generations as she could influence her children with this mindset and this is where you notice patterns in families and you cannot understand where they come from. Patterns like divorce and separation that are running in families. Well, it is not the divorce or the separation that is the pattern here, it is the attitude adopted and the negative perception behind this attitude.

Can you see how perceptions can influence something so profoundly that if you are depending on this perception it can make or break you? This however does not mean all divorces and break-ups are from this scenario.

Reading the above must have taken you back to the belief system and how significant this is to your perception of the world, and indeed it is.

They are not always your own perceptions

As we have seen from the examples above, our perceptions can be learned. Some are learned from parents and other authoritative figures from childhood, like in Raj's case. Some are forced upon us like in Shan's case, and others you learn on your journey, like in Isma's case.

Self-assessment

It is good to undertake a little exercise about your perceptions of things to reassure you of where they have come from and to establish if they really are organic or if they are governed by someone else's perpetual perceptions of the world. The best way to do this would be when you are next faced with a scenario try to really concentrate on your views and perception of the situation and see if it feels organic or if you can see a link with somebody else's perception or a link to a childhood experience. There isn't anything wrong with living a life from a perception of the world that was originated not from you. The only time it is a problem is if this is a negative perception, and above all if it is holding you back from moving on in life, or it is interfering with matters.

Sometimes what you have been told or taught as a child becomes so ingrained in you that you cannot tell the difference if this is your perception or someone else's. Just like you were taught that the lion is a dangerous animal, you then associated lions with danger without a trial. These are things that are taught to us but we know they are correct as the whole world is following this framework. But when it comes to individual or personal circumstances, sometimes it is hard to tell where your perception of a particular thing originated from. When following the little exercise above, you may just be surprised at the links you establish.

Sometimes a perception isn't something that you have learned or one that is prescribed to you. Sometimes people can perceive things in a certain way because they want to conform to what may be expected of them as they may not have the confidence of original thought, as we saw in the previous chapter about interpretation. Original thought can be scary if you have never been allowed it as a child.

Why do we conform in scenarios? You can link this back to your childhood too. As a child, most of the time you knew it was easier to conform to what was expected of you than to speak out against it and get yourself into trouble. When once this was practiced as a child and it worked, the mind automatically ticked this as a strategy to use when unsure if you might get yourself in trouble for saying the wrong thing or that you might make a fool of yourself. Therefore this pattern was repeated and maintained. As an adult, you would be doing this subconsciously so you wouldn't even need to have a thought process to apply this strategy.

Imran's case study

> Imran's parents, according to them, would always be right, even when Imran knew they were wrong. Most of the time, even when Imran knew that what his father or mother was saying was incorrect, he would happily conform. The few times he said otherwise he ended up in a lot of trouble for being bold and disobedient.

As a child it is different, there is little understanding of right and wrong and there is always fear of being in trouble. As an adult you may ask yourself if you have discovered that you do conform, why, and who are you pleasing. You may ask yourself: Am I still being reminded of authoritative figures in my childhood and is that inner child still fearful for what may happen as a result if I try to apply an original thought? Inner child is the child that remains in you, not in a human form obviously, but the child part of you that does not grow up. This child is usually holding all the emotions and feelings experienced as a child, good or bad, now living in an adult body. Assure yourself and your inner child that this was fear in your childhood about something in your childhood and a fear received, processed and endured by a child's mind. You are no longer a child, but still possess that fear, or the inner child still does. This is because habitually we grow up with this subconscious setting that has been applied in childhood. It isn't something tangible and therefore very hard to see and understand. But that was all in childhood. Look at that fear now as an adult with an adult mind and an adult thought process. You will be very surprised how many thoughts and fears you have but do not understand where they have originated from; instead we class them as habitual and they are perpetuated. For example, you may be scared of loud noises; is it because there was too much shouting around you as a child? What about fear of elevators or even heights? Most likely this is linked to something in your childhood that has left you with this fear. Nail biting is a habit, but where did this habit come from? We are never born with habits. Maybe it was a coping strategy when you were nervous as a child. A bit later on we will look at how we can change perceptions into healthy ones.

Sometimes we just conform to be able to fit in out of fear of appearing different. This again should raise the question: Who are you pleasing? If you are not pleasing anybody then there should be no fear. But if you have fear of not fitting in then that usually means you are trying to please. There is nothing wrong in pleasing as long as it is not holding you back from your true potential and if it is not harmful for yourself or anybody else.

Perceptions can be unhealthy as well as healthy

Annie's case study

> Annie's perception of herself was that she was pretty useless at most things. She did not complete her high school education and was quite happy to leave high school and settle for a job in retail. On the other hand, her perception of her older sister was that she is very bright and excels in anything she sets her mind to. While admitting this, Annie showed a lot of resentment toward her older sister too. It transpired that her parents, her mother in particular, always told Annie that she was nothing like her sister. She was constantly told that her sister excels in anything she puts her mind to while Annie is pretty useless at everything. Her sister was usually praised excessively in front of her. Annie was always asked, "Why can't you be like your sister?" This perception of her parents, in par-

> ticular her mother, has impacted Annie so greatly that she holds the same self-perception. This has also had a negative impact on the relationship she has with her sister, or shall we say the relationship she chooses not to have with her sister because of her resentment and jealousy toward her.

Maybe you can relate to this scenario and if so maybe you could ask yourself: Is this is what I really am or do I believe this because I have been told it? Again, this happened in Annie's childhood therefore you can see the huge impact it has had on her and by default that child mind is still the driver of her perception, but it is not too late to change these self-perceptions. If you can relate to this, see if you can link it back to someone or a certain event in your past.

We can all have healthy perceptions

What is a healthy perception and how can you measure it? To know if you have a healthy perception of something or someone is when you can be at peace with it. It is that feeling when you know you no longer feel that bitterness and uneasiness about it. It is when you know it is not about every situation being perfect or imperfect, rather accepting it for what it is with a healthy mind. It is also when you have established that you are seeing the world through your eyes at the present time with your very own perception at this time, with your self-prescribed lenses, equipped with the understanding that perceptions can change and are variable.

Now here is the key to knowing how to change an unhealthy perception of a situation into a healthy one, and I will give you some examples to help you understand this. We all come across people who hurt our feelings, don't we? And we want that one opportunity to tell that person how much they hurt us, we want to emphasize each word and emotion and make them feel bad about themselves for causing us this hurt. So we take the opportunity and go and do this. Did it make you momentarily feel great and high, was it a cathartic release? Did it give you a buzz and a feeling of power? Great! Then what? You were left to feel those same feelings of hurt when they resurfaced from under this glossy buzz that was being experienced momentarily. The person who caused you hurt has probably got on with their life and you are now left not only with your own hurt but the hurt of the hurt that you have just shared with this other person, achieving nothing for them or yourself. This was no long-term therapy; it was like putting a Band-Aid over a cut without examining how deep the cut is. How many times will you put a Band-Aid on it and how many times after removing the Band-Aid will something else cause that same skin to re-open because it wasn't fully healed but actually needed further treatment?

So what is it that really would help in this scenario? The perception being applied above is that so-and-so hurt my feelings and I will do everything in my power to let this person know how it made me feel. Now we know what the long-term outcome will be of that: a momentary high with a long-term outstanding healing required. What is really needed is a healthy thought process to be able to deal with this situation in a healthy way.

Exercise

Take the above scenario of someone really hurting your feelings.

Step 1

The first thing that needs to be done is to acknowledge what you are feeling. This requires honesty on your part. Even if you feel that's nasty to admit, just admit to yourself that this is how you were made to feel; nobody is watching or listening, this is just for you. This acknowledging of feelings and emotions is in itself a mini therapy. A lot of the time we cannot even begin a healthy thought process because we are not being honest with our feelings. You must always be honest about your feelings and emotions. By no means am I implying that this needs to be shared or publicized; what I am saying is just be honest with yourself in private.

Step 2

Once you have established what your feelings and emotions are about a particular thing or person (you could take the example of a friend hurting your feelings), what needs to be done next is to process this emotion you are feeling, whatever it is meaning to you right now (at this point don't worry about it sounding healthy or unhealthy). What I mean by process is digest and understand what it is that you are feeling with all honesty.

Step 3

After the processing is complete, then it is time to judge if conversion is required; this would only be required if after processing you have established that you have concluded an unhealthy perception of the situation. Remember an unhealthy perception would be you not being at peace with it.

Samra's example

> Let's take Samra's example where her fiancé said to her that she was so overpowering and loud-

mouthed when they were arguing. This really upset Samra and subsequently it would have fueled her up for a full-blown argument. This time Samra was ready to apply a healthy thought process because previously after similar augments this would leave her very upset and exhausted. She firstly acknowledged her feelings and understood how strong her feelings were. She wrote them down. She was asked to be specific about how this made her feel. The kind of things she wrote down were: "He has made me feel really insecure about myself;" "I hate him;" "How can he be so horrible to me?" These were her strongest three statements of her feelings, obviously there were more. She was then guided to convert each statement into a healthy one. "He has made me feel really insecure" converted to "Even though he has made me feel very insecure about myself, I prefer him not to say words like he did but I cannot control what he feels about me when we are in a full-blown argument. They are not necessarily feelings about me as a whole but me in this particular argument; they are also not necessarily accurate comments but his perceptions of me and especially a perception of me he creates when we are arguing." Samra also gave herself the opportunity to assess herself regarding this comment in case there was an element of truth in this and, if so, if modification of character is needed.

"I hate him" was converted to "I don't hate everything about him; it is these moments of heated arguments when he makes me feel insecure about myself that make me hate him. I prefer not to feel that I hate him as a whole."

"How can he be so horrible to me?" was converted into "I cannot control what he is saying, even though I would much prefer he didn't say it the way he did, but I do not necessarily need to accept it like this. I know like me he prefers not to have these arguments, and while having them we both tend to bring out the worst in each other." This transformation to a healthy conversion of perception of the outcome of an argument cleared Samra's mind of unnecessary things that would previously lurk in her mind for weeks on end, which was subsequently displayed in her behavior toward her husband causing further problems in their relationship. This shows the power of perceptions.

Annie's example

Another example would be of Annie, where she was constantly told that she was useless and asked why she couldn't be like her sister. This perception of her created by others and which has now become her self-perception needed to be converted into a healthy one to enable Annie to move forward and have peace in her heart. Therefore the comments like "You are useless" and "Why can't you be like your sister?" were

converted into healthier perceptions such as "I am not the way my parents are expecting me to be, but this does not make me useless. This is a label they are attaching to me because I don't fit their criteria of what useful is. However this is their perception and not mine. I feel I am useful in a lot of ways, just not recognized by them. I would prefer if they did not feel this way about me and not say these things to me, however I cannot force them or control what they want to say and want not to say." Also "I am not like my sister because I am an individual, I would prefer not to always be compared to my sister and to be respected for my individuality and my disposition of my character; however I cannot control whom my parents would like to compare me to. Being compared to my sister is my parents' guide of measurement of character and person not mine and I cannot control whom they choose to measure me with."

Once we understand that it is not the actual comment a person makes or says that hurts us – after all, these are words and they are not tangible – but it is how we receive it and subsequently how we process it.

IT IS NOT THE COMMENT A PERSON MAKES THAT HURTS US, BUT IT IS HOW WE RECEIVE AND PROCESS IT

It is the thought process our mind endures that causes us to transform these words and comments into emotions, whether positive or negative emotions and whether strong or weak emotions.

ABC of thought process

A (input) is the actual event, comment or words said that is triggering a negative emotion

C (outcome) the emotion or hurt that is felt by us

So to get from **A** to **C**, surely there is a **B** in the middle?

B (the processor) the mind process that we go through to get from **A** to **B**

B is the area that requires modifying to produce a healthier outcome for yourself and society. **B** is the stage where conversion takes place, and if at this stage we can convert the **A** into a healthier **B** like in Samara's and Annie's example then **C** will be a healthier outcome. This is something that everybody can do; it may seem hard work at the beginning but with practice you will be doing it so subconsciously that you wouldn't believe you were doing it any other way before.

A healthy perception will help you move forward in life without carrying extra baggage. It will help you get through life without being toxic; as mentioned earlier, these toxins can pass on to generation after generation, making the world a very toxic place.

A HEALTHY PERCEPTION WILL HELP YOU MOVE FORWARD IN LIFE WITHOUT CARRYING EXTRA BAGGAGE

CHAPTER 4

THE WAY WE FALL INTO PATTERNS IN OUR LIFE

Do you sometimes wonder why you keep falling into the same pitfalls again and again and why there is always the same pattern being repeated in your life? Right down to the point where sometimes you just know where this is leading and you could predict the ending to a particular episode in your life. This is OK when it is healthy and prosperous, but what if it isn't, what if these patterns you keep falling into are your hindrances in life? That's when you know something needs to be done.

What we portray affects what we attract

Believe it or not, the way we portray ourselves out in the world in front of people can determine what you will receive back from the world. Let's go back to our belief system, where you have adopted a belief about yourself, like in Annie's example.

Annie's case study

> Annie was told that she was useless and nothing like her sister. She adopted this belief from her par-

ents and took it on board and believed this to be true about herself. Because it was rooted so deeply in her, she believed this to be true; she would portray herself with that belief to the world.

You see our behavior translates the contents of our mind, so whatever the mind is breeding will be birthed in our behavior. She would talk in such a manner to support and translate that which was breeding in her mind and her body language would deliver that. This belief in her mind created by her parents and now displayed in her verbal language and body language has started determining where she is going in her life. Her self-esteem is very low and her confidence isn't that great either. This was the obstacle that compelled Annie to believe that she would not go on to do further studies after high school as she was not capable and decided to settle for a job in retail. What if a better opportunity came her way, do you think Annie would go for it or hold herself back because she would not have the confidence? Annie has also attracted a partner who doesn't have a lot of confidence but is a very submissive individual. She attracted likewise, but prefers this as she does not have the confidence or the self-esteem to be able to have a relationship with someone who is strong-minded and holds strong beliefs. This way her partner with this disposition is exactly what Annie wants, so he can be completely subservient to her, and consequently this is one area of her life she can control.

OUR BEHAVIOR TRANSLATES THE CONTENTS OF OUR MIND

Abdul's case study

> Abdul with his very healthy upbringing portrays a lot of confidence and has a healthy self-esteem. This is portrayed in his verbal and body language. He has used this to excel in life and continues to take opportunities where he needs to without holding himself back.

Now as I have mentioned body language above, I just want to elaborate on this. We speak two languages: verbal language and body language. Both are means of converting and translating what we are feeling or that which we want to express into a universal mode of expression. The verbal language is all clear to everybody, which is using a language converted into words to express what we want to say, but what about body language? Did you know your body language can speak louder than your verbal language? You know that feeling when you were speaking to someone and you thought she was very cold. Well, it wasn't because the temperature around her plummeted in your presence or something, but rather the body language she displayed was very cold.

You know that moment when you are out with your parents and you have done or said something you were not supposed to and you know you are in trouble when you get home. Your parents haven't said to you that you are in trouble but their body language has demonstrated it to you, that they are furious with you because you did exactly what you were told not to do. This was body language expression from the parent to the child, which the child understood perfectly well.

This demonstrating of body language is usually done subconsciously although we can consciously do it too; however, whether subconsciously or consciously it is very impacting for the recipient.

Another factor in what we portray to the world is our outlook. When we go out into the world with a positive outlook, we will attract positivity. Why? Because we are displaying this in our verbal and body language. On the contrary, when we go out into the world with a negative outlook and this is displayed all over us, we will attract similar kinds of people with similar outlook. What we forget is that every human being we interact with has the subconscious ability to translate body language and verbal language from their perception and from this a reaction is generated. We as human beings are natural reactors; we react to what we are in contact with. I am sure you can relate to this where you have reacted to someone's anger with anger, or when someone has incited you to be upset, so the stimuli applied caused the reaction by you, for example becoming upset, just as planned. On the other hand, you could be feeling really low and upset about something and coming into contact with a vibrant positive person may just uplift your spirits and provide you with a means to overcome your current misery. It would be good if we could all remain resistant, especially around negative people, but that is not the case with a lot of us most of the time.

The portrayal is coming from different sources

As we have noted above, our belief system plays a very important role in how we portray ourselves to the world and it can impact self-confidence and self-esteem significantly.

As well as the belief system, people around you can influence your portrayal to the world. Let's take a self-harming mother as an example. She has never degraded her children in any shape or form and provided them with all the love and care they needed. The only flaw is she has a habit of self-harming by cutting herself when she dips into deep depression. Even though the love and care was provided by her, this habit of hers can still influence how you portray yourself to the world. Here you are seeing a very loving and caring mother, an excellent role model, yet her self-harming habits accompany this caring loving nature. Therefore through this influence and possibly learned behavior, you may subconsciously display yourself as a very loving and caring individual but have tendencies to self-harm to cope with pressure because this is what you have learned. A lot of the time when youngsters self-harm, they themselves don't know its origin but assume it is a coping strategy they have learned to cope with stress. The positive role model above glossed the negative and destructive influences it carried beneath not realizing that both of these personalities can influence her children especially when it is openly portrayed.

On the other hand, a strong and healthy role model from a mother or father can also influence how you portray yourself. This is because you have learned skills and behaviors from them which are now imbedded in your character, just like the above negative one was too.

The role models around you as a child and even now can really influence how you feel about yourself. This feeling will be portrayed in the two languages - verbal and body language - and displayed for people to read and decide on a mode of reaction to this. This is how reaction is generated from others, primarily through what is portrayed through your language to them. The recipient receives this language and reacts via a mode of response selected. From here we attract people and situations and from here we can receive our answers on questions such as: Why do I always attract the same kind of people? or Why do I always end up in this situation?

To change your situation, you first need to identify your portrayal mode and see if this is where the problem lies.

You may question siblings having similar upbringing, yet having different outcomes in life. Here it is how each child interpreted and perceived their situation to be. Role models are definitely impacting but the level of how one interprets and perceives the role model we can see in the example below.

Nina and Miah

> Nina and Miah are sisters being brought up by a single mother who is a drug addict and tends to

> self-abuse by overdosing and cutting herself. Nina hated her mother and held her mother responsible for her adopting similar habits. On the other hand, Miah would view her mother's situation with compassion and understand that her mother cannot cope and therefore uses these means as a coping strategy. She never adopted her mother's habits, instead this experience gave her the opportunity to understand what can happen in the world for a single parent. She used this negative experience to become a social worker to be able to give back something to the world for all the single parents out there.

This example shows that negative or positive role models do not always equate the same perception for the future as it seems, which is what this chapter is covering. There is an element of personality and genetic make-up that can play an influential factor too.

Self-portrayal impacts the experiences you will have

Rajs's case study

> Raj's experiences with an abusive father have impacted him to the level where it is portrayed through both languages – verbal and body. As you have read earlier, he has subsequently adopt-

ed this abusiveness and it has landed him in a lot of trouble. As Raj continues to portray this in his verbal and body language, he is falling into a pattern of attracting similar experiences. Therefore it is a vicious cycle for him because his self-portrayal would incline him toward looking and asking for trouble which subsequently finds him in trouble.

Imran's case study

Imran has had a few opportunities come his way but would fail at interview stage due to his low self-esteem with added lack of confidence. This low self-esteem and lack of confidence was portrayed in both of his languages which were received and reacted to by the interviewers and a mode of response was selected.

Abdul's case study

Abdul, on the other hand, has welcomed many opportunities in his life: opportunities to excel, and opportunities to explore. This doesn't mean he achieved or accomplished everything he has tried, but nevertheless he has never denied that he was provided with an opportunity. Abdul doesn't like trouble, therefore doesn't look for it hence never attracts it. On a rare occasion when he was bullied, he used the appropriate means to deal with it. Abdul loves opportunities and this is very strongly portrayed in both his languages and he therefore attracts them too.

Breaking the chain

Everything learned can be unlearned: when this philosophy is applied then the impossible can become possible.

Self-assessment

Step 1

Observe yourself (and this can be really fun) and see how you feel you portray yourself. See what your verbal language is saying and also what it is not saying and what your body language is saying. Is change needed? Is your portrayal holding you back? What experiences would you really like to be having? Now when I say this, you have to be realistic; that doesn't mean that you say you wish you would wake up tomorrow morning and own a Ferrari or something. That is a wish and we are not talking about wishes; what we are talking about is what kind of life experiences you know you can have but you are holding yourself back from.

Step 2

Next, question yourself why you are holding yourself back, hopefully you will be able to establish some links somewhere. Don't be upset when you do establish any links, look at it this way: if you hadn't discovered it, how would you have been able to unravel it and move forward?

Step 3

With any links that are established, see if they can be modified using the same exercise in the perception chapter, use this to "upgrade" your self-portrayal.

Always remember that portrayal is of two languages: body and verbal. One is intertwined with the other; no matter how much you try to look at them as two, they are a whole representing what is in your conscious and subconscious mind being acted out for the world to interpret.

Once you can start moving the stones out of your way, you will not trip over the same stones again and again, saving yourself from long-term damage of constant falls and subsequently you will not be having a repetition of negative experiences.

CHAPTER 5

CULTURE PLAYS AN IMPORTANT ROLE IN MOLDING WHO WE ARE

Our parents pushed to implement their culture

For those of our parents who were the first generation in the UK, hats off to them. What they endured coming into a country so different from theirs and having to deal with the culture shock and decide which way forward to go with their children must have been a tough challenge for them that we cannot even begin to imagine.

A different culture must be scary, and for those who were from an eastern background and came to the UK, this was even scarier as there is a considerable difference between the culture they had just left and the culture they had just entered. Being so vulnerable in this new culture, the safest thing to do was to stick to what they knew and to pursue it. The ones who were the first generation to enter the UK were kind of guinea pigs to a trial not tested before, yet we fiercely hold them responsible. Therefore implementing their culture from back home to the maximum was protection for them in this very open modern society.

Their culture was a monoculture

As this change of culture was not trialed and tested before neither was leaving their monoculture trialed and tested before. Their monoculture was practiced by all back home in their country and nobody would do otherwise unless they were willing to face the consequences and be outcast. Their culture was simple (according to them) and applicable in all spheres of life in their country and to them it never proved otherwise. Now when I say culture, I am not referring to religion at all as that is a separate matter because religion can so beautifully unite you worldwide while culture is a separate entity. It is a conduct applied by society to form rules and regulations for the functioning of that society.

Most of the time in eastern cultures, the elders in their society were obeyed whether they were correct or not; the culture was they have to be correct because they are the elders. Even if someone had noticed something incorrect, they would not have the audacity to then voice it, rather out of respect it would just get brushed under the rug. Indeed there may have been some good points about this but nevertheless some negative implications too, especially if something unjust was occurring right under someone's nose and the norm is to condone it.

If children were to speak out, out of the perimeters of what was expected of them by the elders, they were automatically classed as disobedient.

Hisham's case study

Hisham was brought up in Pakistan where traditionally a monoculture was applied. When I say was applied, it's because I am not sure if that is entirely the case now. When Hisham was once questioned by his dad as to why his grades were low in math, the expected response should have been silence, but Hisham built the courage this time to speak out and say his grades were low because he dislikes math and finds it extremely difficult. The fact that he spoke the truth was completely overlooked by his father. Instead two other points stuck out clearly for his father: that Hisham had the audacity to speak out the way he did when under his father's scrutiny and the fact that he made a choice not to like math instigated a serious penalty for Hisham.

This was normal back home in those days, probably not now due to education and media providing the opportunity to look out of the box and learn the norms of other cultures. This was the na-

> tional culture and anything that breached this was looked at with contempt. There was no exposure to multiculture, therefore they did what was appropriate at that time and what they knew as best.

Dangers of applying monoculture in a multicultural society

What does it mean to apply a monoculture to a multicultural society? So let's go back to the first generation parents who entered the UK and continued to implement what they thought would be safe to do.

Let's first take a look at the benefits of this. The benefits were really none other than being able to mold your children into your perfect thought-out model. Nevertheless, this would cause confusion as the perfect thought-out model may confuse the children who are also the generation of children exposed to the western culture. Please don't interpret this as if I am saying one culture is better than the other. What I am trying to put across is which culture works best where, and if applied where it would not work, it could have a counterproductive effect. The result of this would be that it would cause confusion among the children living this kind of double-cultured life and the likely chances are they could rebel. So it's not about denying your culture or your heritage, rather it's about using it and tweaking it to embrace the society that you and your children are currently living in and taking the good from it and applying it.

What has happened is that the first generation, as I have described above, wanted to stick to what was safe and therefore continued to apply their culture to their children who were being raised in the west. This culture was enforced at home and worked perfectly well within the home and family life according to them, although there is evidence to suggest there were problems inside the home too. The problem started when these children started school and were being exposed to a new, different culture. This culture was a culture where you were allowed to speak out and have choices. These were choices of subjects, friends and generally choices where you were allowed to express how you felt about a particular topic or person. Again, this culture worked great for the children because it gave them the opportunity to develop as a person in their own right. There is a respect taught and given in school, which was not always or never seen at home. However, saying this, once again I am not implying that one culture is better than the other as I am sure some can argue that there is a certain amount of conditioning that takes place in schools. What I am trying to show is a comparison in cultures and the impact of being under the influence of the two.

Children being raised by first generation eastern parents at that time were not always offered respect as such as an individual. Instead there was a generic structure in place where the person in authority (parent, grandparent, uncle, aunt or any other authoritative figure) made the rules and the children obeyed regardless. This is where the conflict began, where for part of the day they were allowed to be who they are and have choices, and for another part of the day they had to jump back into the mold set out for them by their parents. This jumping in and out of roles has caused great confusion among children leading them to rebel against their parents.

Be open to the culture you live in

You know it doesn't have to be a bad thing to embrace the culture you live in, instead it could be quite resourceful. This doesn't mean you have to embrace the culture you are now exposed to entirely, rather it means allowing room for adaption and not having fear of the consequences of stepping in. There is more fear in being overwhelmed by a culture and not knowing what to do and trying hard to protect yourself and your family from it. It is probably easier embracing the culture you have now migrated to at your own level of acceptance and requirement and empowering it rather than it empowering you. You are the one in control, not the one being controlled.

YOU ARE THE ONE IN CONTROL, NOT THE ONE BEING CONTROLLED

The other thing people really feared from these cultures was that by being open to another culture and embracing it means compromising their religion. This is not the case; religion remains the same and is so universal that it can be applied to every culture. It is not something that changes, you don't adapt your religion for any culture, and rather you fit your religion within any culture you enter. Your religion will never expire in any society, culture or country.

So it's not the material things that need changing, it's the mentality. It is adopting an understanding about what your children are exposed to on a daily basis and seeing where there is goodness within that which can be applied at home too. It is also about keeping up with the current learning, media and technology advancements so your children are able to talk to you about these things. It's basically keeping up with today in the place you are living in today as opposed to keeping up with yesterday and the place you lived in yesterday, which has already expired today.

The key point here is that if you don't allow adaption then it is your children that will suffer. They are the ones who will get confused and then start to rebel. They could end up getting themselves into a lot of trouble if they start to rebel by expressing this through socially unacceptable means. They are growing up in a society where there is a lot of exposure and availability; they could use this and seek outside what they are not being given in the home.

Finally, for those who were at the receiving end of being parented by the first generation parents entering the UK, please forgive your parents if you rebel against them. They have tried their very best to do what they thought was best. Like I said before, they were like guinea pigs and were trialing something that had never been tried or tested before. We can never imagine how hard it must have been for them, yet we are so quick to hold them responsible.

CHAPTER 6

WE ARE ALL ON OUR OWN JOURNEY

Don't compare yourself to others

Everybody is an individual and has their individual life experiences. It is these experiences that make us who we are. Someone who has had a wealthy upbringing will have a completely different journey from someone who has had a less advantaged upbringing. Just like someone who has been brought up by a single parent will have a different journey from someone who has been brought up having both parents under one roof. Many factors differentiate your journey from another's: health, wealth, upbringing, gender, sibling impact, cultural impact etc. are some of the factors which differentiate our journeys.

We expect others to always understand where we are coming from

This is probably one of the hardest things to accept: when we expect someone to understand our point and where we are coming from, and it can be so disappointing when we realize that we are not being understood or our point of view is just not being seen. However much we expect this from our family, our best friend and our partners, this is not always the case and will never always be the case. I am sure you can relate to these words: *"I have always been there for her but she is never there for me"* or *"When it comes to them, I give everything and when it comes to me, they are never there."* Have you ever wondered why this is the case?

It is not always possible for people to see things from your perspective or understand where you are coming from. Our minds are limited to our experiences which we have had since childhood and are stored in our mind. Even though we may have the knowledge of so many things and exposure too, this doesn't necessarily mean we have experienced it all. What we have not experienced, we cannot understand in its entirety. Yes surely the theory is understood, but theory has to be practiced to understand it totally. Therefore what you have not experienced, you cannot understand fully, even if you claim to. We have seen poverty around the world transmitted through TV all our lives, but those of us who have had an opportunity to visit these places and experience it first-hand know that experiences affirm what the eye has seen and the ears have heard.

Now that you have hopefully understood perception and interpretation, you will understand that when we are being understood by someone, we are being understood from their perception, their interpretation and their experiences, which are all combined to make an analysis to understand the matter in hand. Therefore it is not a case of her/him/them not understanding you; it is a case of them understanding you within their own limitations.

Sarah and Simran

> Sarah once complained about her friend Simran, saying that when Simran has a problem, Sarah is there for her totally and helps her figure things out and console her. She added that when she has a problem herself, she feels she can't rely on Simran for two reasons: firstly the advice she gives is nowhere near the advice she needs and secondly because Simran starts avoiding her as if she doesn't know how to handle her. Sadly both of these assumptions of Simran were correct, not because she wasn't a good friend, in fact she was a brilliant friend, a very generous one too. She would never hesitate in giving money to Sarah and supporting her in many other ways; however, Sarah acknowledges this but the problem doesn't lie in Simran's generosity, rather it lies in her emotional support.

What transpired from this relationship was that Sarah was brought up in an unprivileged background, having to fight to get her way, while Simran was brought up mollycoddled, had a wealthy background and literally was handed everything on a plate. Can you start to see the picture? You can be the best of friends, the most loving sister, the best of couples but that does not mean you, your partner, friend, husband or brother will have the same emotional understanding. It is your life experiences that shape your emotional understanding, your interpretation of matters, your perception of the world etc. Simran is a really good generous friend but that does not mean she has the same emotional knowledge as Sarah. She tried to give the best advice to Sarah in her times of turbulence within the capacity of her emotional knowledge. She found Sarah's problems a bit overwhelming, not because the problems were so great, but rather that Simran could not quite handle them as she just didn't have the understanding to do so. She could also sense slight frustration from Sarah with her lack of understanding hence decided to just avoid her to save herself the embarrassment.

So next time you encounter something like this, where you are really confused as to why so-and-so just does not get you, take a deep breath and relax. They are not meaning to do this. As a matter of fact, they are probably really struggling to be the best they can, but again the best they can be is within the boundaries of their experiences in life, which has provided them with the perceptions and interpretations they have.

Understanding your journey

Have you ever sat back and thought: *Where am I going, where have I come from and where am I now?* Or are you just moving on in life in a robotic fashion ticking all boxes completed on the way and just hovering over the ones you are unable to tick because you are procrastinating.

When I say journey, I am not implying your spiritual journey.

Are you happy with the journey you are on at the moment, if not why? I am sure you can fit into multiple categories, e.g. I am a mum, a doctor by profession, a sister, a daughter, wife, auntie etc. We wear many hats: some hats we have chosen, some we have inherited and some we have picked up on the way and just kept them, and that is fine. But what if you are not happy with the journey you are on?

A time map is a brilliant way of establishing your experiences up to now and you may just surprise yourself when you look at this map. What I mean by this is you may be surprised by how much you have achieved on the way on your journey – or even the opposite: that you still have many goals outstanding that you would like to achieve. Don't let the fact that you still have things or goals outstanding be the reason for putting you off doing this; there is even more reason for doing this to establish what has been done and what needs doing. I class this as being positive rather than being negative because you are accepting what has happened and accepting what still needs to happen and from there take steps toward these goals.

Self-assessment

Step 1

What are your goals, do you have any? Goals don't have to be really big. Sometimes what stops us from setting goals for ourselves is the misconception that they must be big. Of course they don't have to be. If one of your goals is "I will try to smile more" or "I would like to start reading" that is fine. If they were bigger goals like "I want to take up a course in something" that is fine too. It is not about the size of the goal, it is about what the goal means to you and the difference it will make to your life.

Step 2

Once you have written a few goals down, have a good look at what they are. Are they genuinely your goals or goals that have been expected of you? There will always be some goals we have in our lives which are expected of us, like achieving a good level of education or eventually having a good job/career. But these are not the goals I am talking about; the expected goals I am talking about are the ones that came from your negative belief system and have held you back somewhere in life and not let you fulfill your true potential. This is what you have to be aware of, the goals which are stemmed from someone else's mindset.

Imran's case study

> When Imran was once asked about the goals in his life, he said he didn't have any. When he explored a bit deeper with the help of a few exercises, he identified that he actually wanted to be a policeman. Excellent. However, when this was explored a little deeper, it transpired that this professional goal wasn't even his; it was something his father had expected of him as a child and hence got ingrained in his subconscious mind, making him believe that this was his choice all the time. With his upbringing, it was hard for him to even write simple goals for himself, but after some hard work, Imran decided from his own mind that he would like to go into computing, for two reasons:

because he was good at it and because he had enjoyment from it.

My journey

Hopefully, you have now understood that your journey and the journey of the person next to you have never been the same and will never be the same. This is not a bad thing; rather it helps us understand why we can be so different in our understanding, yet so close in nature or love. It also helps you understand that sometimes people don't mean not to understand you the way you want them to or expect them to. It is because they have not had the same understanding of life and experience as you have and vice versa. This does not make anybody a bad person. Don't be upset when you are not being understood entirely by your best mate, your partner or a sibling; they are trying their best from the knowledge they have based upon their individual life experience and journey. If you feel that you are there for everyone but no one completely gets you, then give yourself a pat on the back because that is a unique quality to have, and it is because of this quality that you recognize deficiencies in others. Be gentle on others, they have not seen what you have, they have not experienced what you have. Their journey has not been your journey and your journey has not been their journey, even though you may be on the same journey together now as friends or partners.

Living someone else's journey

What if you are living someone else's journey? Have you ever thought about this? Is your journey really yours or are you trying to live a journey of someone you secretly admire or idolize? Have you ever thought why people do this? We can so easily mock those that do this but don't quite understand why. Most of the time it is because the person whose journey you are trying to live encompasses the qualities in which your journey is deficient.

Sonia's case study

> Sonia has realized that she has not really been living her life as her own journey; instead she has been living a journey of one of her cousins, which she was completely unaware of. Her cousin Layla (older than Sonia), has been an inspiration to Sonia all her life. Sonia had a lot of insecurities in her life and family life at home was pretty much dysfunctional most of the time. What she saw in Layla was how she envisaged her life to be; she also admired Layla's personality. Before she knew it she was so engrossed and self-molded into this journey that she actually believed this was her personality and her journey. At times, she would subconsciously

give Layla the cold shoulder because she began to believe that Layla was stealing her ideas and was imitating her. This was not the case; rather Sonia was so engrossed in Layla's journey that she could not distinguish between herself and Layla.

What transpired when Sonia came for therapy was this mixing up of journeys; she was shocked at what was happening. She admitted how much she admired Layla, to the point of jealousy and resentment. Sonia felt that she didn't know who she was anymore as this had taken the best part of her life. She was reassured that it was not the end of the world; there is nothing wrong with admiring a person and their life, however the danger lies in when you are not admiring but have actually switched and started living the life of the one you admire.

The essence is not in the admiring; the essence is taking the qualities that you admire about somebody and applying them in your life. We all have deficiencies in our life and we see others that appear so fulfilled in theirs. However, we are all on our journeys too. When admiring someone to such an extreme level, always remember that it's not the role of that person that you have to adopt but rather the ingredients of what you admire of that person and see if you can apply this to your life. You will never truly live your life until you understand you are on a journey and so is everybody else, and no two people's journeys can ever be exactly the same.

THE ESSENCE IS NOT IN THE ADMIRING, THE ESSENCE IS TAKING THE QUALITIES THAT YOU ADMIRE

Your experiences, whether positive or negative in life, have shaped who you are. Love yourself for what you have been through. Some things you could control in your life and other things you had no control over. Accept that what has happened has happened and don't be hard on yourself, this will only hold you back. It is time to forgive yourself and move on. Sometimes we are too hard on ourselves; be gentle with yourself, especially now after coming this far reading this book and uncovering things that you probably never thought of before.

Take a good look at your journey. Set yourself goals, goals which are set by you for you. What are your interests, are these realistic, where can these interests lead you to? If they are not realistic, is it because they are taken from someone else's life which is beyond your reach? Well, we know the answer to that which is take the element and essence from it and apply it to your life.

Once you can understand that we are all on our own journeys, this can impact profoundly on our interpretation, perception and understanding of the world.

CHAPTER 7

A HEALTHY EMOTIONAL VOCABULARY HELPS US TO EXPRESS OURSELVES

Did you ever think that vocabulary can play a role in our mold? Sounds a bit weird and shocking, but the truth is that it can make a positive difference that incorrect vocabulary can hinder.

Expression is important

Expression provides you with the freedom of relief and the ability to carry on in life in a healthy manner. When you can express things in a healthy accurate manner, this will stop you from holding on to things that just linger in the mind and create unnecessary and uncalled for problems. Imagine feeling like a free spirit without that unnecessary baggage of voices hovering in your mind about things you wish you had said, or things you did not know how to tackle and deal with, or that you wish you had worded something better because it just did not get the message across that you intended. Many things are left unresolved and misunderstood when the correct emotional vocabulary is not applied. We take this very lightly and sometimes say things because it is the expected correct way of saying things rather than what we really feel. When I say this I do not mean you go and tell someone how much they are annoying you and how life would be better without them, even though that may be the truth. What I am saying is that there is a healthier way of expressing this annoyance where you will feel relieved and the recipient will also have benefited and learned from your expression. Can you imagine how many toxins we could save the world from if there was not so much bad energy in the air, but rather a natural process of healthy expression?

You may be wondering why this is so important and why a chapter is needed for it. We are human, and our natural way of expression is, as mentioned before, through two languages: body and verbal. Here we are covering the verbal part. Talking is one of the biggest means of communication and probably a high percentage of what we say is a load of rubbish. Sometimes we talk just because it is sociable, or to reduce the silence that has just fallen into a room, or even to make ourselves look confident when in fact we are feeling quite out of place and really uncomfortable. We talk at work, at home, on the phone, to ourselves and children.

Going back to our molds, perceptions, experiences, interpretations and journeys, these all have a role in the kind of vocabulary we use to express ourselves.

What is not expressed is suppressed

Have you ever wondered where what you haven't expressed that needed expressing is at this moment? I can tell you right now that it is suppressed somewhere in your mind, in your subconscious. Indeed, some things have to be let go and that is OK as not everything can be expressed. But verbal expression where there is a recipient involved is not the only type of expression there is. It is not only about expressing to a person but also your expression about a situation or a person to yourself. Having a healthy emotional vocabulary isn't just for other people; it is firstly for you, to allow you to understand yourself. To understand why you did or said what you did or behaved in the way you did. I class this as the most important expression of emotions, even over the expression where a recipient is involved. When you can be clear and honest with yourself, you have just paved yourself a healthy pathway to begin to be able to express yourself easily to others, and this will clearly show in your portrayal.

Damages of suppression

When your mind has too much clutter, the clutter will spread out into different areas of your life causing too many obstacles and interference in persevering in life in a healthy manner.

Raj's case study

As a child, when Raj watched his father being abusive day in and day out, he could not express what he was experiencing to anyone else. But also as a child he could not contextualize what was happening and therefore could not even form an understanding healthy enough to be able to deal with it. It was a part of his life he decided to bury because it had no significance to him when he became an adult, although we know the impact it had on him by turning him into an abusive person. This later played a role in his marriage where he could only express himself physically, either lovingly or violently, as that is what he observed and absorbed as a child and therefore adopted. There was always clutter in Raj's mind which kept him swinging between the two extremes of love and violent expression. If he had been able to express what he was feeling and understanding with a healthy emotional vocabulary, that would have stopped his wife asking for a divorce because she could not handle the "split personality" that she was dealing with on a daily basis. (Does this label "split personality" sound familiar, ever thought where it may have come from?) She claimed she loved him and understood he loved her too; however, this was not a sufficient recipe for a healthy marriage. She explained that Raj was volatile and she never knew if she was coming or going with him. Raj blamed his wife for being the extreme one and said she was the one who didn't know how to handle a marriage. After both of them had therapy, it transpired that Raj, as we know, was an abusive person due to his childhood. This did not make him a bad person, he just didn't know otherwise. His emotional vocabulary did not exist; he expressed all his emotions physically as that is what he learned to do as a child. Therefore right from childhood up until now, he had a lot of clutter in his mind which he did not know how to deal with, which built up and was expressed in a fashion he had learned, not knowing the dangerous plants that were growing in his mind. He was taught through therapy how to use appropriate emotional vocabulary to express what he needed to. This took a lot of time to break through but thankfully the marriage survived.

Syed's case study

Another example is Syed, who lost his father when he was three years old. He was told his father had gone to Pakistan for a holiday. Syed waited and waited and knew this was not the case. He knew he was lied to because all the crying and mourning at the time did not correspond to this but he was too young to understand what was happening. He also understood that he had to live out this lie and pretend that he believed what he had been told. He had been taught how to lie. Without going off on a tangent, but as I have mentioned lying, I cannot help but point out that we are the first to teach our kids how to lie by telling them a lie. In Syed's case he was told a lie and felt he had to live out that lie too for fear of getting into trouble if he told anyone that he may know the truth. The way this impacted his life was that Syed never expressed what he was feeling truthfully as he had to live with this lie and subsequently mapped his life to accommodate and perpetuate the lie. Unfortunately, he became a compulsive liar and started living his life in this way. This affected his relationships with people, as he would lie through his teeth to get through life. The funny thing is, he never lied to abuse systems, rather he lied to hide his true feelings about matters. He was told a big provisional lie as a child which was never modified and subsequently he believed this was the way you get through life. Just like Raj, Syed also had an unhealthy emotional vocabulary – in fact an emotional vocabulary didn't exist. It was as if his emotions got blocked the day he started realizing that his father had died and he was being lied to. The strange thing is he doesn't remember exactly when this happened, but gradually the death of his father which occurred when he was three was later talked about in front of him. It was as though he was now allowed to know but still wasn't told straight out and there was a subliminal assumption on the part of others that they knew he knew the truth. This made things no easier for Syed as his subconscious mind had accepted the fact that he was not allowed to know the truth, so he never spoke about his father or his emotions. He suppressed all these emotions from the point when he was lied to and he knew it was a lie but understood he had to live out this lie. It would have taken Syed just to admit to himself that even though he was lied to, he was hurt and missed his dad and maybe decide that one day he would talk to his family and explain what he knew and the implications of their actions. But as humans, we don't know when things are causing an effect most of the time, and when we do realize an effect has been caused we don't usually establish a link to the roots of this effect.

We all know suppression of any kind will explode at some point. But this is not the kind of suppression we are talking about here. The suppression we are talking about is where something has been suppressed at such a deep level in our subconscious mind that we are unaware of its implications in all areas of life. Unfortunately, this suppression will perpetually drip out throughout life in everything we do without us realizing this is happening, handicapping us from our true potential.

You might think that I am asking you to get the dictionary out and start using the right words with the right meanings; I can assure you this is not the case, you do not need to use or swallow a dictionary at all! What I am talking about is firstly putting words to your feelings and this is primarily done alone with yourself. They do not have to be big words from the Oxford dictionary; what I'm asking is for you to name your feelings and name what that feeling is meaning to you and how it is making you feel. This may seem like a pointless exercise at the beginning but it can be very impacting and fruitful in the long run. Now don't tell me that you can't think of words, not today where technology has advanced to the point where we communicate less verbally but more via email, SMS, Facebook and WhatsApp etc. This is all done with the use of words. Therefore before your expression is channeled out to others through words, start with yourself. This is done by you starting to put words to the feelings and emotions. You may even surprise yourself. This isn't a one-layer exercise; there may/ will be many layers.

Example

You are angry with your boss; start the exercise by:

- *Asking yourself why you are angry and start using words to explain your answer to yourself.*
- *Next you can go another layer down and that is to ask yourself how this is making you feel – again you will describe this in words.*
- *There can be so many layers, like: How could I have avoided this? or maybe: How I could have not said that certain thing. It all depends on the situation. Sometimes you may not even need to go down so many layers, just exploring a few layers, and using the appropriate vocabulary will help you understand yourself and your feelings.*

You will actually feel better. Just by using words to describe your feelings can help alleviate half of your suppressed emotions, yet we underestimate this exercise so much.

When you have mastered this with yourself, it is then time to express yourself to others in a healthy, respectful and appropriate manner. When I say healthy, respectful and appropriate manner, I mean that it will benefit you and make you feel better about yourself, and as a result you will pass this positive energy to the person who is receiving this expression from you.

Once all the layers have been explored and you can form a healthy and polite enough expression then this is the time to build the confidence to be able to express it. We use disrespectful and inappropriate language when we don't know correct ways of expressing. Once you start applying this correct format, it will provide you with the confidence and tools for expressing to others what it is that you really want to say. This will stop the usage of inappropriate language that will not achieve anything and will take you back to square one where the cycle will start again about why you said what you did and why you didn't say something when this was what you really meant. Save yourself from this unnecessary time-consuming disease, instead spread the energy of a healthy emotional vocabulary.

SPREAD THE ENERGY OF A HEALTHY EMOTIONAL VOCABULARY

CHAPTER 8

EMPOWER YOURSELF TO CHANGE THE MOLD

We all have the ability to change

Did you know that anything that has been learned can be unlearned, and this applies to bad habits we learn? No one was born with habits, perceptions and interpretations, our life experiences have shaped these. What we are born with is the ability to have perceptions and interpretations, but how we do it and from what angle is all from our experiences and journeys, as we have seen. But first you must be willing to embrace the change.

Let's start off by disposing of what you are not happy with and I know this can be difficult because we are talking about a non-tangible matter here: the mind. But this non-tangible matter is far more impacting than probably anything tangible you possess because this is the matter of your mind and your mind is with you wherever you go and whatever you do.

Self-assessment

- *Take one of your characteristics and view it; it could be the way you talk to people, the way you listen to people or maybe the way things make you feel.*

- *What is this characteristic doing for you? Maybe you could weigh up its pros and cons. We could take as an example confidence issues or anger issues; by now, after reading this book, you would have more or less identified its origin, which most likely was a learned habit or a coping strategy. See what this is doing for you, write down the pros and cons.*

- *Once you have established what this characteristic is doing for you, then the choice is yours to dispose of it or to perpetuate it.*

The choice is yours but at least you know that you have the tool there to use. You can do this with all your characteristics. Take your time with each and don't rush through; if done properly it could have fruitful impact.

Danger of not changing

As I said, the tool is there for you to use and only you can allow this change. It is a good idea to see the flip side of not changing something that might be working against you and this is that you will continue to fall into the same experiences in life and the same question – Why me? – will be with you for the rest of your life. You will also reduce your chances of living your life to your full potential by holding yourself back with a perpetual vicious circle that you cannot get yourself out of. As discussed earlier, this toxic development will pass down from generation to generation polluting the world even more. If we look around at some of the problems in the world, where do they originate from? They are primarily from the mind, whether it was an original thought of the one committing a crime or a learned thought or even a coping strategy. All of these are potentially dangerous when used in a dangerous way. Do we want generation upon generation of individuals who have confidence issues, anger issues or any other negative quality that will hold them back from achieving their full potential in life?

Why do people commit crimes or even socially unacceptable behavior? The possibility lies in that their crime or behavior is used as an expression of something that is suppressed so deeply in them that it is expressed in a socially unacceptable way. It could stem from possibilities like being a victim of childhood abuse, neglect in childhood, attention seeking (we think only children seek attention when in fact adults seek attention on a different scale). I am not siding with people who commit these crimes but rather providing an insight of what may be going on behind the scenes.

The longer we leave our debilitating molds, the more potent they become. They subsequently spread the pollution or toxins in all areas of our lives, and before we know it we believe this is how our life is. We will use every excuse to blame anybody in our lives bar us for the situation we are in.

The question of why this always happens to us will remain because our situation will not change until we take the first steps of making that change. We will continue to remain in the situation or the lifestyle we have until we can identify where change is needed and then how to make that change. Anyway, you know you want to change, otherwise you would not still be reading this book. There must be something that has resonated with you that has compelled you to keep reading.

Benefits in changing

The biggest benefit that a healthy change can provide you with is the ability to be able to move forward in life with love and understanding of your past and all those unanswered questions. This subsequently can lead to new discoveries, new doors opening, new experiences, new relationships and much more. There also comes a relief of not holding anyone responsible for your situation and if there is still a part of you that wants to hold someone responsible for a part of your life, it could be done with a new revelation and understanding, and hopefully with love.

As I have suggested in this book, forgive yourself for feeling how you have been feeling up to now, forgive yourself for the anger, hurt and resentment you have had inside you which others have been the victim of, and forgive yourself for the choices you have made that you now understand were not entirely your authentic choices. This is all in the past now, but the only way forward is to make that peace with your past. Forgive others too and move on as most of the people who have played a role in your molding did not mean to have the impact they did. They themselves were probably victims of other people's molding and also victims of other people's negative belief system. If you were to create a family tree just on this matter, you may be surprised at what you learn about who may have been influenced by whom and who was a victim of whom etc. But I want you to be completely clear on the understanding that nobody meant to have a negative impact on you. Everybody did what they thought was the right thing at the time and what was the right thing for you.

If you were a victim of anger and abuse, most of the time this wasn't a planned attack on you or on your subconscious mind, rather it was the fact that the perpetrators did not have the understanding or the ability to be able to make that change to stop this pollution spreading down in generations to come. This is with the exception of the few who cause deliberate premeditated harm.

The buzz out of this would be that you did it; you unlocked that potential and have decided to make that positive change, not just for yourself but a change which will have a bigger impact and that is to the world: one fewer toxic individual. New experiences will open up for you, as now your mind has had a complete detox of toxic molding. Now the ideas, thoughts, perceptions and interpretation will be organic and completely yours. Your past experiences will still play a role in this, no doubt, but in a conscious light rather than subconsciously.

Sheila's story

Sheila was in the corporate world and required therapy for confidence and self-esteem issues. When she put her head down to make a significant change to her life by following this kind of therapy, surprisingly five years down the line she is no longer in the corporate field, instead she is now a palliative care nurse.

Raj's story

After therapy Raj is now a successful youth worker. He wants to work with young people and make a difference to them at a young age before the toxic molding gets the better of them.

Only you can make the change

The one thing that pops into our mind when we think of this kind of change is that it is too late, the damage is done. "No" is the answer, it is never too late to change. The brain is capable of making new neurons all the time – therefore how can it ever be too late?

Make the difference for generations to come, let us invent positive belief systems and positive learned behavior. This is an achievable goal and starts with you taking the first step. We have immense potential but tend to hold ourselves back. But the good thing is now you have discovered how to make that difference.

Sometimes it can feel tiresome trying to make changes alone and you can lose motivation doing so, but honestly that one person will impact another who will then impact another and it can go on. Not just that, the peace that it will bring inside you is what the true gem is in all this.

The magic question that you need to ask yourself is: If my mold was something I had no control over, is changing the mold something I do have control over?

IF MY MOLD WAS SOMETHING I HAD NO CONTROL OVER, CHANGING THE MOLD IS SOMETHING I DO HAVE CONTROL OVER?

CVVCV

ABOUT THE AUTHOR

Samina is a qualified hypnotherapist and psychotherapeutic counselor who has a humanistic approach to her therapy which is reflected in this book. She has been invited by her local community to deliver cross-cultural psychological related talks. She herself has grown up between two cultures, having a Pakistani background and growing up in a British culture.

Lightning Source UK Ltd.
Milton Keynes UK
UKOW04f1842200914

238848UK00001B/2/P

9 781909 623675